S0-AGP-671

Even in death, Stone wanted no recognition. In a Theodora Kroeber poem he left to his son, he wrote:

"When I am dead, cry for me a little. Think of me sometimes, but not too much . . . Think of me now and again, as I was in life, at some moment which it is pleasant to recall. But not for long."

HARD WORDS AND OTHER POEMS

Books by Ursula K. Le Guin

NOVELS

The Beginning Place
Malafrena
Very Far Away from Anywhere Else
The Word for World Is Forest
The Dispossessed
The Lathe of Heaven
The Farthest Shore
The Tombs of Atuan
A Wizard of Earthsea
The Left Hand of Darkness
City of Illusions
Planet of Exile
Rocannon's World

SHORT STORIES

Orsinian Tales
The Wind's Twelve Quarters

FOR CHILDREN

Leese Webster

POETRY AND CRITICISM

The Language of the Night
From Elfland to Poughkeepsie
Wild Angels

HARD WORDS

and other poems

Ursula K. Le Guin

HARPER & ROW, PUBLISHERS, New York

Cambridge, Hagerstown, Philadelphia, San Francisco,

London, Mexico City, São Paulo, Sydney

1817

HARD WORDS AND OTHER POEMS. Copyright © 1981 by Ursula K. Le Guin. All rights reserved. Printed in the United States of America. No part of this book may be used or reproduced in any manner whatsoever without written permission except in the case of brief quotations embodied in critical articles and reviews. For information address Harper & Row, Publishers, Inc., 10 East 53rd Street, New York, N.Y. 10022. Published simultaneously in Canada by Fitzhenry & Whiteside Limited, Toronto.

FIRST EDITION

Designer: Sidney Feinberg

Library of Congress Cataloging in Publication Data

Le Guin, Ursula K   1929–
    Hard words and other poems.
    I. Title.
PS3562.E42H37 1981   813'.54   80–8210
ISBN 0–06–012579–9   81 82 83 84 85 10 9 8 7 6 5 4 3 2 1
ISBN 0–06–090848–3 (pbk.)   81 82 83 84 85 10 9 8 7 6 5 4 3 2 1

CONTENTS

I. WORDHOARD

For Karl and Jean

Consider the action of writing
short lines as the action
of grabbing at straws, of drawing
as hoping you draw the long straw,
of carving as bringing the world
to be by short hard repeated
blows; consider the act
of considering as will to continue
to be. The old violinist
has crossed the gulf of the decades
on a highwire of catgut. Consider
the lovely devices of living
to which we are driven, driven.

Wordhoard

The dragon splays her belly on the gold,
Gross hoarder, hot-eyed miser,
Holding all the earth can give to hold,
And none the wiser.

Dumbness deadness darkness is your nest.
Brooding there, fierce booby,
No fire's enough, not even in your breast,
To hatch a ruby!

Why keep such glory in the glowering dark,
Pent and unspent in earth?
Give me one coin, one diamond-spark,
One kingdom's worth!

I will not give a single pearl, says she,
Stretching a switchblade leg.
The one I gave would prove to be
My own, my Egg.

So filch your treasures frightened and alone,
Pickpocket, miserable thief,
The anger opal and the honor stone,
The gold of grief,

The joy star and the emerald despair:
Take them up to glitter in the sun,
Bright and worthless: earthfast in my lair,
I keep that one.

Danaë 46

God of the gold rain,
the room is cold;
will you not come again
to me old?

God in the bright shower,
it grows late
in the room in the tower
where I wait.

O the shining terror
of the first embrace,
the eyes, the arrows
of your eyes, your face!

The window is open.
I have set the board.
One spark, one token!
I am mortal, Lord.

The Man Who Shored Up Winchester Cathedral

He was a poet, a knight, he wore
that supple somber armor
and the great staring helmet
that screws your head on tight.
He lumbered, gorilla, Goliath,
to the coping, and over
to slide down out of sight.

Out of mind.

Down there you go lightly,
lightly in darkness.
They lower the bags of cement
that flutter and waver like feathers,
like birds in invisible hands.

You work there by touch.
You touch the foundations
in the old darkness of waters
under the earth. Under mind.
Your breath
only escapes to the surface
in hurrying strands.
It's silent.
You're drowned alive, blind,
forgetting, forgotten,
alone, you're there
alone, the foundations are rotten
holding ten thousand tons of stone.

When you come up to daylight
the cathedral stands.

Invocation

Give me back my language,
let me speak the tongue you taught me.
I will lie the great lies in your honor,
praise you without naming you,
obey the laws of darkness and of metrics.
Only let me speak my language
in your praise, silence of the valleys,
north side of the rivers,
third face averted,
emptiness!
Let me speak the mother tongue
and I will sing so loudly
newlyweds and old women
will dance to my singing
and sheep will cease from cropping and machines
will gather round to listen
in cities fallen silent
as a ring of standing stones:
O let me sing the walls down, Mother!

Translation

As you get older
hard things mean more,
soft less, maybe.
You can read granite:
Renounce.
Diamonds? Get ready.

Dead languages.

You can read water.
Now what?
Walk on it?

Drink, sweet lady.

The Mind Is Still

The mind is still. The gallant books of lies
are never quite enough.
Ideas are a whirl of mazy flies
over the pigs' trough.

Words are my matter. I have chipped one stone
for thirty years and still it is not done,
that image of the thing I cannot see.
I cannot finish it and set it free,
            transformed to energy.

I chip and stutter but I do not sing
the truth, like any bird.
Daily I come to Judgment stammering
the same half-word.

So what's the matter? I can understand
that stone is heavy in the hand.
Ideas flit like flies above the swill;
I crowd with other pigs to get my fill;
            the mind is still.

The Marrow

There was a word inside a stone.
I tried to pry it clear,
mallet and chisel, pick and gad,
until the stone was dropping blood,
but still I could not hear
the word the stone had said.

I threw it down beside the road
among a thousand stones
and as I turned away it cried
the word aloud within my ear,
and the marrow of my bones
heard, and replied.

Hard Words

Hard words
lockerbones
this is sour ground

dust to ashes
sounds soft
hard in the mouth

as stones
as teeth

Earth speaks birds
airbones
diphthongs

More Useful Truths

O stones help me
give me bread

Bread break my
    teeth

Teeth tack my breath
down on my tongue

Tongue run away with me
stumbling on stones

Willow O save me
sweet silly willow!

Words are to lie with
    believe me
    believe me

The Writer to the Dancer

Shifty Lord let me be honest
Let me be honest shifty Lord

Let me go sideways sideways
Let me go sideways shifty Lord
there is doors Lord doors
opening sideways

II. THE DANCING AT TILLAI

The Night

This is Kālī's day
the woman in my sleep
said This is Kālī's
day

     O Mother please
please Mother children weep
let it not be till tomorrow
the little children say

There is a woman drumming
until the drumhead breaks
until the maiden wakes
and sees the coming day.

Mother takes the fear away.

Night is Kālī
the god appears between her thighs
stands in beauty, dances, dies.
     O Mother, comfort me.

Śiva and Kama

Look up, look out! Desire
comes to adore you,
over the April meadow.
White, white his flesh is,
silver his laughter.

Uncover your third eye,
burn him to ashes
that he may cast no shadow
being with you and before you
hereafter and forever.

Epiphany

Did you hear?

Mrs. Le Guin has found God.

Yes, but she found the wrong one.
Absolutely typical.

Look, there they go together.
Mercy! It's a colored woman!

Yes, it's one of those relationships.
They call her Mama Linga.

Why does Jesus always wear a rag?

I don't know; ask his mother.

Carmagnole of the Thirtieth of June

I will grow fingernails
to scratch the scab
that stops the sore's lips on the scream
the pusty whistle of escape
EEEEEeeeooooooo steamboat annie comin roun the bend
I will grow fingernails
ten feet long and walk on them like stilts
& breathe steam out my nostrils
& split boards with my eye
                    HAI!
don't get near me with your martial arts
unless you want to get split right down between the balls
neat as a colonel's chicken
            I got Real Bad Vibes
I have been talking to my father
who died in 1960
he's 101 years old not feeling very perky
he gets left out of things
locked out.
                I will grow fingernails
and claw down the Lubyanka
stone by stone by stone.
                        Yeah. Sure.
Listen, my vibrations are so bad
they're Richter 8.7
look out down there in Daly City.
My toenails are growing too.
I can dig up graveyards with them

and dance on the burning ground.
I use the urns for footballs
& my tongue hangs out a yard.
I am WUMMUN, ta doody boo-bah,
but even worse than that I'm me
and feeling mean.
           God's stomach
rumbles like a drum
when I jump on it
when I dance on his chest he snores
when I dance on his gut he farts
when I dance on his cock he comes
when I dance on his eyes he wakes and all the stones fall down
           ashes, ashes
all fall down.
           Get up and dance, creation!

School

The Dancing Master advances
with propriety, stepping neatly.
Elegant sobriety.
Admirably suave.

O my God! His zipper!
What is that thing? A cobra?
It wags at me so sweetly.
Quick! Put it back inside!

Cummerbund won't cover it.
Nothing hides it completely.
Black tie and gaping pants,
the Dancing Master laughs.

They say he uses cannabis.
I wouldn't trust my daughter
at his school.
       O but how sweetly,
sweetly he can dance!

Middle

When the pure act turns to drygoods
and the endless yearning
to an earned sum,
when payday comes:

the silly sniveling soul
had better run
stark naked to the woods
and dance to the beating drums.

Turning, turning,
call the dance out, master,
call out the silly soul.
Curtsey to your partner,
do-si-do.
Call out the comets, sister,
and dance the Great Year whole.

The only act that is its end
is the stars' burning.
Swing your partner round and round,
turning, turning.

Tale

Where did I get this middle eye?
So you can see me clear.
Where did I get these extra arms?
To hug me with my dear.

What have I got these big teeth for?
Bite off my head my sweet
And dance upon my body
There where the rivers meet.

A Semi-Centenary Celebration

O my terrible darling
I never could dance
I am afraid of tigers
and in love with god

It's time to put your foot down
SO: O Arthur Murray
couldn't do it better
Ginger Rogers Fred Astaire

My anger seeks a lover
so little Joanie Yoni
found lovely Louie Linga
but it's all esoteric
and strictly in the head.

CHORUS

Strictly in the head.

And so I learned to tango
and waltz and play the sitar
all at the age of fifty
and everybody laughed.

I am in love with tigers
and afraid of god.

CHORUS

You too can have a personalised brahman!
33,000 choices!
From 2 to 30 arms!

When you make love to tigers
they eat you
when you make love to Sambhu
they call it bestiality

or is it vice versa
if you are at the moment human

I will never abandon logic
or lovely Louie Linga
says Mrs. Micawber sobbing.

So I tiptoe through the tango
and my necklace-skulls get tangled
with the strings of the veena
and everybody screams.

O my terrible dancing darling
O my dear dirty Louie
do you know who I am?

I am the dance you're dancing
I am the loving tiger
I am the hungry god

You are the drummer, you are the drum
but I am the sound of drumming

Paśupati

When I think of the herdsman my heart
grows heavy with tenderness.
Let me lie with the lord of sleep
in the bed of the waters.

His hair is never combed.
He dances in the mountains.
The old men
say he's crazy.

A river falls out of the stars
into his hair
hiding the moonlight.
He dances at the crossing
of three rivers
the Ganges and the one beneath the Ganges and the one
that falls out of the stars.

His are all waters
the levelness of waters
the silences the depths.
He's naked, his hair is grey with ashes
hiding the shining crescent.

O my lord I Parvatī know myself
daughter of the king of mountains
immortal, when my heart grows heavy
with tenderness thinking of my husband the herdsman
who never combs his hair.

Drums

Sun dance
stone dance
bone dance
one dance

sky dance
bird dance
word dance
I dance

The Dancing at Tillai

I said the center
was a ring of stones
a hearthplace.
           I meant a place for bones
and ashes.
        Crib, carseat,
bed, park bench,
target center for the neutron bomb
or passed away in sleep at 93
there, and there, and there
is the center and the burning ground
the hearth the heart

and no circumference.

They burned Shelley by the sea
There was Tillai
His heart burst noisily
That pleased Kālī

They burned Hiroshima
There was Tillai
The blood burned painfully
That pleased Kālī

I seek comfort, mother.

Find it in the ashes.

I seek comfort, mother.

Find it in the bones.

Mother, I am sick at heart.

Come to the drumming at Chidambaram.

Mother, I am sick at heart.

Come to the dancing at Tillai.

Do you hear the drumming, child?
Do you see the fires?
See where my lord bears drum and flame
his right hand says Be not afraid
his left hand points to the dancing foot
he dances in the heart laid waste
the burning place
river and moon are in his hair
his lifted foot is grace
his lowered foot is sleep
he dances in the center
there, and there, and there,
all time, all space,
the arch of all the stars
contains his splendor.

Come to the drumming at Chidambaram
child, child, child,
come to the dancing at Tillai

III. LINE DRAWINGS

At Three Rivers, April 80

A tree that blossoms in the wilderness
in some April beyond history
and farther west than all the pioneers
is in no way less
though there be none to bless
and no woman stand in tears
under the whitening flowers.

Only the tears were ours.

Slick Rock Creek, September

My skin
touches the wind.

A lacewing fly touches my hand.
I speak too slow
                for her to understand.

Rock's warm under my hand.
It speaks too slow
                for me to understand.

I drink sunlit water.

Smith Creek

Ripples of water quicken rippled mud.
Ripples of light run downstream
on opal-blue and brownish minnow-depths
to flood in foam across a sunken branch.
Mica in mud says Sun, staring and shining,
but the creek ripples, goes forward, seaward,
counting aloud the ten thousand things,
carrying heaven downward.

Torrey Pines Reserve

For Bob and Mary Elliott

Ground dry as yellow bones.
A dust of sand, gold-mica-glittering.
Oh, dry! Grey ceanothus stems
twisted and tough; small flowers. A lizard place.
Rain rare and hard as an old woman's tears
runnelled these faces of the cliffs.
Sandstone is softer than the salty wind;
it crumbles, wrinkles, very old,
vulnerable. Circles in the rock
in hollows worn by ocean long ago.
These are eyes that were his pearls.
                                One must walk
lightly; this is fragile.
Hold to the thread of way.
There's narrow place for us
in this high place between the still
desert and the stillness of the sea.
This gentle wilderness.

The Torrey pines
grow nowhere else on earth.

Listen:
you can hear the lizards
listening.

Coast

In bed in the first salt light
with the east ear I hear birds
waking and with the right
Ocean breaking inward from the night.

Ted with Kite

Slight soul in windy fog
tugs to soar
high on the double line
over the shoreline
checked, jerked, windjoy,
windthing, struggling
till the boy's hands are sore.

Central Park South, 9 March 1979

Crystal shoulders of Manhattan schist
break the recalcitrant and littered ground
inside the heavy coping, and I think:
my father saying that the island's all
schist, fundamentally, and we laughed.
And did he walk here as I walk
between the weary horses and the trees,
but he was ten and I am forty-nine,
in 1886, cap and bare knees; more likely he
ran, on the paths there, by the lake.

For Mishka

Who gave me an Angora shawl
from pre-Revolutionary Russia

The goats of Orenburg,
the ghostly goats of cobweb,
walk in procession on the snow
between the izbas of Orenburg.
The snow shows through them
and their eyes are ikons.
They are going slowly
towards Oregon.

Richard

Loyalty bound him. Not deft,
not flexible. Stanley betrayed him.
Why did he fight so hard to die
so sorely hurt? Did he foresee
the hump, the murders, and the theft,
the withered hand, and all the Tudors made him?
That were the sorer wound.
He lived what he was bound to be,
an honest man; a king, like any man;
son of a dark year; bereft.
He dies hard. *Loyaulté me lie.*

Morden Lecture, 1978

A tall winter oak
Peter Medawar
his left side paralysed
for nine years, "the mind
does not have boundaries"

his work took him past
where they said the walls were

alte terminus haerens

I see Lucretius as a tall grey man
waiting to say hello to Medawar
somewhere across the wall
for there is one wall

Everest

How long to climb the mountain?

Forty years. The native guides
are dark, small, brave, evasive.
They cannot be bribed.

Would you advise
the North Face?

All the faces
frown; so choose. The travellers describe
their travelling, not yours.
Footholds don't last in ice.
Read rocks. Their word endures.

And at the top?

You stop.

They say that you can see
the Town.

I don't know.
You look down. It's strange
not to be looking up; hard to be sure
just what it is you're seeing.
Some say the Town; others perceive
a farther range. The guides turn back.
Shoulder your pack, put on your coat.

43

From here on down no track,
no goal, no way, no ways.
In the immense downward of the evening
there may be far within the golden haze
a motion or a glittering: waves,
towers, heights? remote, remote.
The language of the rocks has changed.
I knew once what it meant.

How long is the descent?

North

North in the shadow of rocks
clear water falling forward
under my shadow and shadow of rocks
and the low thin sunlight falling

Landscape, Figure, Cavern

A stone leaning
on its shadow.

The sun seen
from a distance.

Stairs going downward
from the fourth mountain.

Mica. A dry stream. Silence.

Why does she carry a jar on her shoulder?
She glances back once.

Narrow feet like a horse's pasterns
step on their own shadows.

Distant glittering scattered
in sand. Under dark hair.

The Journey

For Joseph Needham

After the fifteenth turn Si Ho
began to sing like a whistle.

We carried the falcon cage on poles.
My father always said to me,
My son, when will you learn?

They use wicker for their cages here,
having neither wood nor bronze.

Three fifths of life. My friend Lo On
died on the eighteenth turn.

Kish 29 IV 79

To the Owners

Prince, my rock is blue-green serpentine:
it lends itself to clay.

Crossing the creek in the first place
I will walk where the others walked,
though my feet are heavier
than the hooves of deer.

Did a girl walk here
a long time since?
What did she carry?
What did she wear?

Lady, my flower is the yellow broom,
not native to this place.

Winter Downs

For Barbara

Eyes look at you.
Thorns catch at you.
Heart starts and bleats.

The looks are rocks
white-ringed with chalk:
flint fish-eyes of old seas,
sheep's flint-dark gaze.

Chalk is sheep-white.
Clouds take shape
and quiet of sheep.
Thorn's hands hold stolen fleece.
The stones sleep open-eyed.

Keep watch: be not afraid.

IV. WALKING IN CORNWALL

1. *Chun*

The first day: to the high place of Chun.
The road goes low between walls
of spark-strown granite, dry-laid
by those who cleared the little fields,
and kept up since, for maybe eighty generations:
heavy boulders earthset as the base,
smaller rocks set close and vertical.
Gorse breaks gold from roots among the rocks.
The road stinks, till we get past
a farmer turning muck on his high field.
The farmyard drive's all liquid mud. Then no road,
only a grass track up the hill
and up, and wind a bit, and all the while the land
rising in long green swells wave-netted by the walls
that mark the oldest fields in England,
and up, onto the land into the wind,
until we realise that this shallow ditch
between rockheaps and gorse and heather clumps
is the outer ring, and we have come to Chun.
　　　　The inner ring still stands. Dry stones.
There are some roofless rooms. The heather bells
are last year's, dry and snakeskin-frail.
A lark goes up and up and sings and sings
over the fortress of the sea-wind.
Two big stones mark the gateway,
and the wind drives bright between them,
king of the castle, coming home.
　　　　　　　　　　　　The well

waits. Clear water under rocks,
slipped coping-boulders, knots of weeds.
A hilltop spring, that made the place
defensible, a living-place: the life of Chun,
secret and perfectly clear. As clear as breath.

    We made a little offering to the spring,
eating our picnic: a bit of pastry and an apple core:
you offer to such places. Then you hope
they know it wasn't meant as litter.

    Straight on from the standing stones
of the northwest gateway, past the view
to Morvah and the dull gleam of the sea,
over the granite backbone of the land
to Chun Quoit. Here's a grave turned inside out.
They set the stone slabs up, set the great roofstone on,
laid the bodies in the room of rock,
piled the earth all over in a mound,
a rounded barrow. And grass and gorse and heather
grew over all, no doubt. But roots
have trouble holding, in a wind
that blows across five thousand miles of sea
for twenty centuries. The covering earth's
all gone, the bones are gone; the grave
itself stands up, grey granite in the wind.
There's not a soul, there's not a sound.
Sun's gold on the old stones.
Lichen is lovely, grey-green, violet, gold.
Clouds drift and pile up, grey, grey-blue, and white.
They pass on southward on the wind
over the high place, over the old place,
the rock-wall rings, the grave, the shallow well.

Chun is a name
in a tongue that no one speaks now
but rocks and larks.

2. *Men-an-Tol, the Nine Maidens,*
   Dingdong Mine, and Lanyon Quoit

We passed Woon Gumpus Common on the left.
You can't go everywhere,
even when it's called Woon Gumpus.

Four Americans straggling on a heath.

The track's a dry streambed. Little signs
point softly, rain and weather-faded,
whisper: Men-an-Tol.

>   The ring is in the valley
>   the door is in the valley
>   the valley is the mother
>
>   Round door
>   open mouth
>   hollow thing
>
>   Time passes through time's circle
>
>   The mother wears this ring
>
>   What is the marrow of this bone?
>
>   Down in the hollow valley
>   come be born
>   of stone

O it is the quietest place,
the shallow valley, Men-an-Tol.

Then up again and through the buckskin bracken
and March blows blithely off the prancing ocean
and makes all noses run, and up we go
and find nine maidens where the map says none:
old maidens, low and lumpy; some have fallen,
some got staggering drunk in 99 B.C.
Small maidens, very old, not saying much.
    On past them; and the topmost crest and spine
of this hard granite ridge, this skin-on-bone,
this high-and-dry place, turns to bog:
the springs rise everywhere. Boots squelch.
We hop from gorse to tussock,
and so arrive at where the map says nine,
and there they are. We count them as eleven,
or maybe twelve. Maybe you can't count them
twice the same. You can't be sure of maidens.
And when they dance in rings in early March
in lonely places, you must count the sun
among their number.

            Ring around the sun O
            Sun among the ring
            Nine and nine are one O
                So stones sing.

    So on we go and up and overland
a little farther to the sober thing,
the upstart and admonitory finger,
the chimney of the tin mine on the hill.
It's made of the same stuff as Chun,
the Maidens, Men-an-Tol, but not in rings:
These stones are cut, cut square,
and set to stay there, grand the building, and it stayed,

though all the shafts have sunk in, dimpled pits,
and you can only guess at where the wheels worked once,
the noise of iron gears, the sluice's rush,
the glare of smelting, women sorting ore,
men who used to sweat here underfoot,
down in the hollow places in the dark.
All quiet now, up here; all gone to grass;
the tin mined out; the miners have gone home.

The Isles of Tin, the Misty Isles!
"It was not certain," Caesar says, "that *Britannia*
existed, till I went there."

Nothing is certain, Caesar bach.

Nine maidens sort the misty ore
at full moon in the shadow of the tower.

On down and down now, through the pasturelands.
Ten young heifers (is it nine? or twelve?)
stare with the eyes of anxious goddesses
and heave warm, muddy, ruddy flanks
in sighs as we go by, excuse us please
for walking through your pasture to the Quoit.
This one is Lanyon. We have left cut stone
a thousand years ahead of us again.
Lanyon's so big you can walk under it.
The stones have soaked up sun and are as warm
as heifer's flanks. Once it was chilly here,
and dark, under the barrow; but the barrow's gone,
the wind blows through the sunlit tomb.
All's dry and clear and clean. You cannot count
the years. Counting means nothing here.

Measure a ring's length, count the sun!
Can you weigh emptiness?

The valleys are shallow
and the hills hollow
at the triple ring of Chun
at the ring of Men-an-Tol
at the rings of the Nine Maidens.
The empty mineshaft and the open grave
are full of sunlight
and the wind is sweet as honey in the mouth.

3. *Castle An Dinas and Chysauster Village*

The next day: off the humping bus,
up past the quarry. Danger!
Blasting: Weekdays at Noon.
White sandhills, lunar; then a gulf, a gap.
A big blast it was made that one—
a hole so big you see the ocean through it.
Hurry on by, they might just blow us up.

There on the top of things is Roger's Tower.

Who on earth was Roger? Bishop, prince?
Landgrave of Ludgvan? Emperor of St. Erth?
Why did he build his Tower? No one knows.
It looms up here for miles, a great keep,
a mighty ruin on the vaulting hill;
you get there, and it's all of twelve feet high.
Never was higher. Four fat little turrets
complete its whole ambition.
Two men might fit inside it,
if they had not been eating Cornish cream.
Around behind it, ruinous,
and breaking into yellow gorse-flame everywhere,
the rings, Chun's sister, Castle An Dinas.
So here's the Bronze Age, and in front of it
the Middle Ages. Here's the granite walls
(boulders for base, small stones set vertical)
and here's the granite walls (cut square, set true).
And who were they? and who was Roger? who?
the wind says to the heather.
Elegant, the arch above the door.
And no one knows what Roger's Tower's for.

Place is three fourths of Time.

So we went down, and missed the muddy path
across the fields, and trudged along the road
for decades, and the back of my right knee
objected, ligament by ligament,
and Theo lagged, until the brindle cat
of Little Chysauster Farm came out and purred
and wanted to be petted till the cows came home,
which cheered us up; and we went on, and climbed
past stone-walled fields, zigzag,
hungry and hot and tired, and came home.

It was home, once, Chysauster village was.
Nine families, their cattle, their hearthfires.

O small cold hearths, so old, so old,
yet you could light a fire in them tonight.
It would be the same fire.
We don't need very much:
water and warmth and walls, the flickering ring of faces.

There is a room as round as any coin
and filled brimful with sunlight.
That was a woman's room, I think.

The roofs are off, the wooden walls are gone,
the centerposts are gone, but not the hollowed stones.

There was a spring ran through the half-walled court
of one of the nine houses, in a chute of stone.
The spring went dry. No sound but wind.
Although you kneel beside the little hearths

you cannot hear the arguments,
the stories, or the snores on winter nights.
But if you sat a while in the round room
you might hear, I don't know, you might—
a woman singing to a sleepy child.

A woman singing softly. Now and then.

The laughter of my children
far off among the ways among the stones.

The laughter of her children.

And the wind as sweet as honey in the mouth.

V. SIMPLE HILL

Simple Hill

As I went over Simple Hill
I saw a woman dancing:
Give it away, away, away,
Give it away to the west wind.

The wind came blowing off the sea
and set the ash trees dancing:
Give it away, away, away,
Give it away to the grass stems.

The grass bent downward to the stones
under the wind and whispered:
Give it away, away, away,
To the feet of the dancing woman.

As I went under Simple Hill
I saw my daughters dancing.

At a Quarter to Fifty

At a quarter to fifty the clock struck
Lost, lost, in a sweet voice,
Lost, so many times
that I lost count, and so believed,
and came to live in the house of grief.

The Child on the Shore

Wind, wind, give me back my feather
Sea, sea, give me back my ring
Death, death, give me back my mother
    So that she can hear me sing.

Song, song, go and tell my daughter
Tell her that I wear the ring
Say I fly upon the feather
    Fallen from the falcon's wing.

The Indian Rugs

I swept the floors on All Souls' Day,
making the clean wood clean.
I laid the rugs down in the bedroom
for winter, for the warmth in winter,

rugs woven by women in exile
long ago in those cold mountains,
the mountains of Colorado.

You walked on them as a child,
dear soul, as a little child,
on the clean wood floors of your house
in the mountains of Colorado,

for the warmth, for the warmth in winter.

Cavaliers

I have gone to seed
and the cavaliers ride through me
flicking the feathery grasses
with riding crops
     fastidious.
I am all burrs and tarweed.
     O desolation!

We Are Dust

We are dust in pain.
The light shines through us
as through wave-spray, dust of water
breaking, or the falling rain.

THE WELL OF BALN

1. *Count Baln*

I am a nobleman of vast estate,
girthed like an oak tree.
I own the oldest forests, oak and ash,
and the mountain lakes
where swans in autumn beat the wind to storm
unseen by other hunters. I am heir
to the house of seven hundred rooms,
its cornerstone the Standing Stone of Baln.
My heart beats slow and sound as a great bell.
But in the center of my house and heart a hole
is round and blacker than my beaver hat
and deeper than mines, deeper than roots of rivers.
And all the leaves and diamonds and hounds
fall into it, the hours and eyes and words,
the closer that I clutch them sooner gone,
and disappear. I lean above the well.
I call and gaze. No star, no stir.
Dry it goes down, dark and dry.
No rope, no bucket. No echo of my voice
or any voice. The hollowness
and the long dark stone way down.

I have let my candle fall into the well.
I have fired my hunting rifle into it.

Nothing shone or stirred or ever will.

What is the use of being a nobleman?

2. Baln's Wife

Why does he go there with his gun,
his old dog, or the sack
of rentgold from the eastern villages?
Why does he go into that room?
An empty cellar like a prison cell,
no door, no chair, no crucifix, no window,
bare. He goes in and he shuts the door.
I heard him speak aloud.

He came out without the gold.
I never saw the dog again.
He did not speak to me that day
nor look me in the eye that month.
In the dark early morning in our bed
I felt him shaking, but he did not speak.

If I knew what he feared!
I have searched that room on hands and knees
praying. There is nothing there.
Nothing stored; the bare floor;
nothing, nothing to fear.

3. Baln's Daughter

I have been down that well a hundred times.
I used to play with children with white hair
in one of the countries down inside the well
where all the rocks are glass.

If you turn to the side too soon
you get in the blind tunnels.
White birds, white bulls without eyes.
You have to go on down.

If you go down and down,
the person in the boat on the slow river
in the dark place said,
you will come clear out at last.

I crossed in the boat instead.
I paid the boatman with my father's gold;
he laughed and gave it back.

I like the country on the other side.

Totem

Mole my totem
mound builder
maze maker
tooth at the root
shaper of darkness
into ways and hollows

in grave alive
heavy handed
light blinded

Amazed

The center is not where the center is
but where I will be when I follow
the lines of stones that wind about a center
that is not there
                    but there.
The lines of stones lead inward, bringing
the follower to the beginning
where all I knew
                    is new.
Stone is stone and more than stone;
the center opens like an eyelid opening.
Each rose a maze: the hollow hills:
I am not I
                    but eye.

Self

You cannot measure the circumference
but there are centerpoints:
stones, and a woman washing at a ford,
the water runs red-brown from what she washes.
The mouths of caves. The mouths of bells.
The sky in winter under snowclouds
to northward, green of jade.
No star is farther from it than the glint
of mica in a pebble in the hand,
or nearer. Distance is my god.

Tui

Life is easy for the youngest daughter.
Her name is Tui, little fish in water.
Her brothers tease and praise her.
She is obstinate and lazy
and quick-hearted. She and her mother
talk for hours together.
"I'm going to catch that minnow,"
her father says, "and fry it in a pan
with parsley." She laughs, she darts away.
Her life is easy and her name means Joy.

Vita Amicae

For Jean

When you were rain you fell
when you were cup you held
when you were whole you broke
   loud, loud you spoke
   when you were bell

When you were way you led
homeward until the end
when you were life you died
   live, live, you cried
   when you were dead

Uma

Look there. So, here: hear her,
Beginning's daughter.
She sings to stones.

Clear water running
in a handhollow.
You do well to fear her.

There is no sweeter singing.